PETRA
A DOG FOR EVERYONE

Biddy Baxter
and
Edward Barnes

PELHAM BOOKS

By arrangement with the
British Broadcasting Corporation

CONTENTS

Introduction		6
1	How it all began	7
2	Petra grows up	12
3	Petra's puppies	20
4	Enter John Noakes	51
5	Four generations	53
6	Peter and Petra	57
7	Petra and Daniel	62
8	Bathing the dogs	66
9	Death of Patch	69
10	Arrival of Shep	71
11	Famous faces	74
12	Death of Jason	79
13	Birthdays	80
14	Petra retires	82
15	Goodbye Petra	88

BLUE PETER

Introduction

At ten o'clock, on the morning of Wednesday, 14 September 1977, a mongrel dog called Petra died peacefully at her home in Sussex. She was 15 years old. The following day there were pictures and obituary notices in all the national newspapers, and every news bulletin on radio and television carried a report of her death. She was mourned not only by her owner and friends but by six million children throughout Britain and by millions of adults who remembered her as part of their childhood. By the end of the week, 20,000 letters of sympathy had been received in the Blue Peter office.

Who was the owner of this remarkable dog? Some would say it was Peter Purves of the Blue Peter programme, or even the Governors of the BBC. The truth is that she was owned by all those millions of people who were saddened by her death.

She was a dog for everyone.

How it all began

On the last Blue Peter programme before Christmas 1962 Owen Reed, who at that time was Head of Children's Television, appeared on screen with a large cardboard box covered with Christmas paper and ribbons. He solemnly presented the box to Christopher Trace and Valerie Singleton (it was long before Lesley or Peter, or even John Noakes!) who cut the ribbon, removed the lid and revealed for the first time a tiny 8 weeks old brown and black mongrel puppy.

Of course, many television programmes had featured dogs before that day. There had been several series about bringing up puppies, grooming and training. But this was going to be different.

Right from the start, Petra was going to be part of the team. She would appear on *every* programme, not just the ones about dog training. When Chris and Val went out and about with Blue Peter film cameras, Petra went along too – whether it was a day by the sea, or an archaeological dig, or skiing trips to Scotland, or to watch amazed whilst Chris and Val took off in an air-balloon. Like a good family dog, she always seemed to be there.

We wanted all those children who weren't able to have a dog of their own to feel that

Petra was *their* dog. And 1,191 Blue Peter's later, the children of some of those children still expected to see Petra on every Blue Peter programme.

She was called Petra not by the Head of Children's Television or Chris and Val, but by popular vote. In those days the programme was only once weekly and the audience was not so vast as it is today, but even so, 10,000 cards suggesting dogs' names poured into the Blue Peter office: "Petra" emerged as a clear winner.

Petra very soon knew what was required of her in the studio. She would make straight for the special "raised bit" of the studio set which was designed so that we could get good shots showing her sitting next to Chris and Val. It didn't take long for her to know when she was "on camera". Just before transmission she would be lying down apparently fast asleep, but as soon as she heard the drum roll that starts the Blue Peter signature tune she would sit up and look bright and interested. But truthfully, her favourite tune was always the one at the end because she knew that meant escape from the studio and a run in the park.

Chris and Petra with her dog-training certificate of merit.

Petra grows up

The training of Petra was very important. If this was going to be a dog for everyone, it had to be a well trained, well mannered dog that could be taken anywhere without being a nuisance or an embarrassment. There is no magic formula in producing a well trained dog. It's just common sense, hard work and patience.

We wanted everyone to join in the struggle, to suffer our frustrations when things went wrong and to share our triumphs when they succeeded. Blue Peter has always been a "live" programme – with no chance to do it again. So when in one training session Chris solemnly said "Stay" to Petra, turned his back on her, and walked the length of the studio, five million viewers saw her get up and waddle after him long before he realised it himself.

We were lucky in having Angela Mulliner as our dog advisor. She took over the whole course of instruction for Petra. She supervised her diet as well as her training; and the fact that Petra lived to such a ripe old age must in some way be due to Angela's care when she was a puppy.

We thought it would be a lovely idea to make a film of Chris, Val and Petra having a day out by the sea. The date was fixed for the first Wednesday in May when the weather ought to be good. The location was Camber Sands, the nearest sandy beach to London. The sea, however, is a very long way from road and the beach being flat and sandy is very exposed.

This didn't worry Petra in the slightest. She thought that the beach was invented just for her pleasure. She raced along the dunes, dug enormous holes in the sand and dashed in and out of the sea, despite the cutting East wind. Chris, however, didn't share her delight. He didn't have a nice brown coat like Petra's, and soon his chest became the same shade of blue as his swimming trunks.

Petra's first visit to the seaside.

"Have you nearly finished?" He asked through chattering teeth.

"Just one more shot will do it and then you can get dressed," said the director.

"I'll need to re-load," said the cameraman.

The assistant cameraman began to look shifty.

"I'm afraid I've left all the film in the car," he eventually confessed.

We looked towards the road where we could just see the car roof gleaming across two desolate miles of loose sand.

Petra came bounding out of the sea, placed her rubber ring at Chris's feet, gave two piercing barks and shook herself all over him. We don't think he's forgiven any of us for that treat by the sea to this day.

At the beginning of 1964 we had a letter from

a little girl called Bridget Scott. "Dear Blue Peter," wrote Bridget. "I know you've got a mongrel dog who is very nice – but how about having a thoroughbred cat?"

We couldn't see any argument against it, so on 25 May a basket of kittens appeared on the programme, and Val lifted out Jason who was to become as distinguished among cats as Petra was among dogs. Petra was not all that delighted at first, which you could well understand. What self-respecting mongrel dog wants to share the limelight with an aristocratic Siamese cat?

It would be a lie to say they became firm friends. After an initial lip-curling and fur-pricking, they settled for mutual toleration. Bored indifference on one hand and lofty disdain on the other. Everything was all right

so long as Jason sat still or walked. When he made the mistake of running, instinct took over and Petra would chase him just like any other cat.

There were tremendous scares during those early days. When Petra was only a year old, the vet told us that she was not a physically strong specimen and couldn't be expected to live long! Even more terrifying was the incident that happened one day when Angela was bringing Petra from her home in Marlow to the Blue Peter studio. They arrived at Paddington Station, and all went well until someone dropped a suitcase just as they were passing the engine. Petra took a nose-dive down the crack between the train and the platform and ended up underneath the engine, which, to our everlasting gratitude, was stationary.

We were lucky, too, in discovering that Petra was, in the first place, highly intelligent, and in the second, very anxious to please. We did several sessions of "Sit and Stay", retrieve, and distance control in the studio and in the park just behind the Television Centre. Petra and Chris got on very well together, and we were delighted with her progress.

By the time Petra was 9 months old, Angela decided that it was time that Petra and Chris went to training classes. "Why?" we asked. "Because it will do them so much good to meet other dogs and handlers," she replied.

In the long run she was probably right, but initially Petra hated all the other dogs, and Chris wasn't exactly knocked out by the handlers either.

There was a large aggressive black Boxer called "Yogi" (stupid name for a dog we thought) who walked just behind Petra in the ring. Yogi seemed to think that the command "Sit" was a heaven sent opportunity to bite a piece out of Petra's ear. Petra, who was always a peace-loving dog, would dive for refuge under the nearest stack of chairs pulling Chris after her.

The instructor was a large lady with a commanding voice and very sensible brown brogues. Her commands of "Forward Handlers", and "Handlers – throw your articles," have been by-words in the Blue Peter office for the last fourteen years. But we learned a lot from those training classes. They helped Petra to concentrate and introduced her to the hazards of strange dogs which stood her in good

stead with all the thousands of dogs she was going to meet in the Blue Peter studio; and they gave Chris the confidence of knowing that he was doing the right thing.

At the beginning of 1965, when Petra was 2 years old, Angela Mulliner thought it would be a good idea if she had some puppies. We agreed, but first we had to find a mate for Petra. Angela told us how important it was to find the right dog to be the father. It would obviously be silly to choose a Yorkshire Terrier or a Great Dane, but there was more to it than that. Petra's mate had to be the right temperament as well as the right shape. Petra was inclined to be nervy and easily scared, so a bold confident dog would be the most likely to produce a litter of lively puppies.

We found five likely dogs, all of which would

Petra's training taught her to ignore strange dogs.

have been all right. They were:

Tonto – a lovable but rather wild Bull terrier

Triska – a Border Collie of high intelligence and obedience

Whimpey – a smooth haired terrier

Luke – a soulful looking golden Cocker Spaniel

and

Bellman – a sturdy looking Beagle.

We thought that as Petra belonged to the viewers *they* should decide on her mate, so we put it to the vote once again.

All five dogs appeared on the programme. It was like the Rose Adagio in the ballet *The Sleeping Beauty* when the suitors are presented to Princess Aurora. Chris discussed each one and the viewers were invited to send in a card to choose the mate for Petra.

The response was enormous – and we had to recruit armies of people to open the mailbags and sort the cards into piles. On the very next programme the outright winner, Bellman the Beagle, was declared.

He and Petra were duly mated, and we all sat back to await the results. After a fortnight Petra looked and behaved very much the same, so on Angela's advice we took her to the vet. He made some tests and shook his head: "I'm afraid there's nothing doing," he said. "I can't believe it," said Val, "not after all those cards and everything."

"Well," said the vet. "All I can tell you is that the bitch is not in whelp – and what's more I doubt if she ever will be."

Petra's puppies

It was only after we'd given up all hope of Petra ever producing puppies that the unexpected happened! It was all quite by chance, too.

A friend of Angela's owned a 4-year-old Shetland Sheepdog. Physically and temperamentally he and Petra were a good match, so we raised no objection when it was suggested that Moss and Petra mated.

After we'd heard the accounts of the meeting of the two dogs, we were even less optimistic. Apparently Petra displayed not the slightest interest in her would-be mate until the very end of the afternoon. Then – during a sudden downpour of rain – the dogs disappeared and were found soaked and bedraggled mating in the garden.

Always an individualist, Petra wasn't going to be pushed into motherhood until it suited *her!*

We were determined, however, not to raise viewers' hopes too high. Being a mongrel, we didn't know very much about Petra's background. She'd never looked particularly robust and, after the failures with all the other mates, we weren't at all sure that she was capable of having pups. But she was. And Thursday, 9 September 1965, became one of Blue Peter's most important anniversaries, when Petra gave birth to eight puppies at half past three in the afternoon.

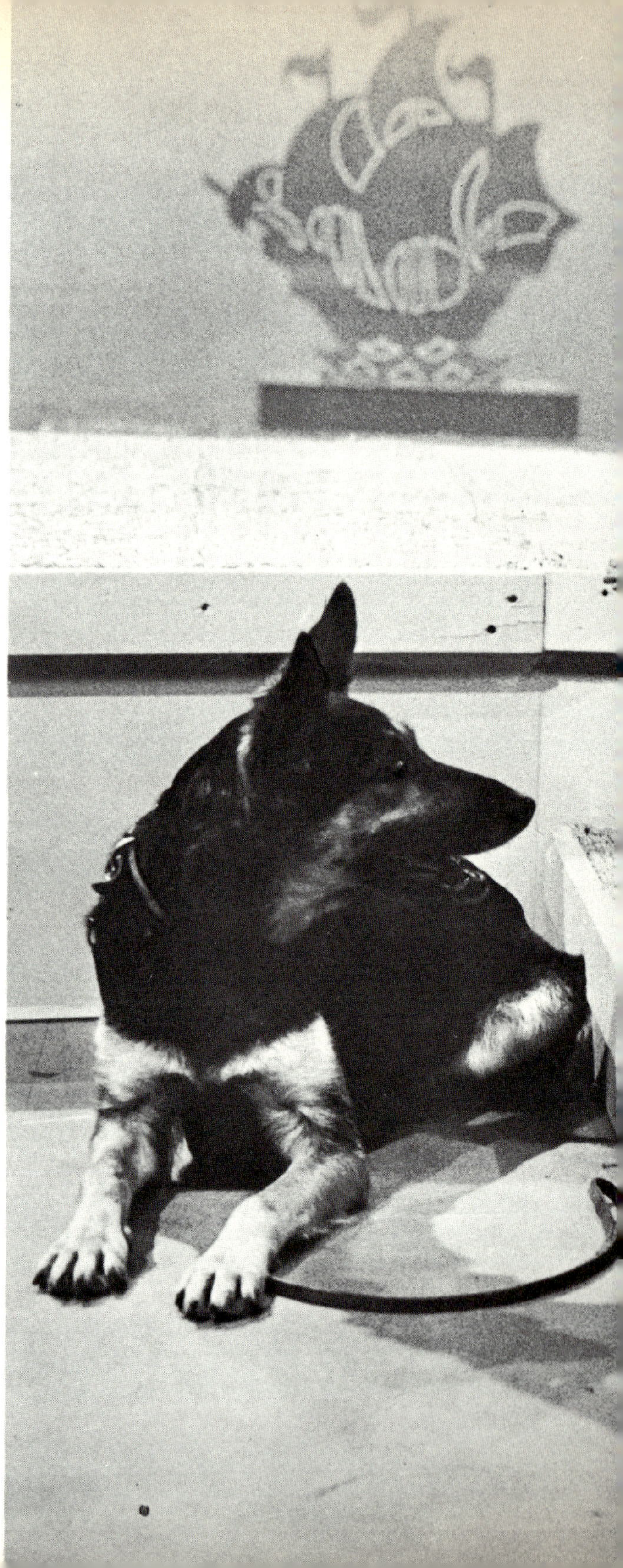

Petra and Moss with their 12-day-old puppies.

Pups at 3 days old.

All eight were healthy and all but two weighed thirteen ounces. There were seven dogs and one bitch. Four of the puppies were black and four were brindle coloured. Two were long haired like their father and the rest were smooth coated like Petra.

It's difficult to describe the impact the puppies made. Blue Peter has hit the headlines on numerous occasions since 1965. Before then newspapers weren't keen to run stories featuring children's television programmes. But as Blue Peter was the first television programme ever to have a dog as a star, it was natural for the

pups to be newsworthy. Even so, we were quite unprepared for the flood of enquiries from the Press. Reporters rang the office constantly and all the national papers demanded photographs.

Twelve days later, when the puppies first came to the studios, Petra had her first-ever press call. We halted rehearsals to allow hordes of sober-suited photographers to drop to their knees (in some cases their stomachs) and vie with each other for the best shots of Petra and the pups with Valerie and Chris.

The next morning Petra and her family had been given a double-page spread by the *Daily Express* and large photographs appeared in the *Mirror*, *Sun* and the London *Evening News*. The Agencies sent photos to all the provincial papers, so Petra's first press call resulted in a file of pictures and stories half-an-inch thick.

But the reaction from the Press was nothing compared with the reaction from Blue Peter viewers.

Once again, we had another massive post. Letters and cards arrived by the sackfull, especially after Val and Chris announced that just as Petra's name had been chosen for her by viewers, so would the pups'.

In the end, to be fair to the hundreds and thousands of people who thought of names, we decided to choose the most popular which were: Candy, Patch, Peter, Prince, Rover, Rex, Bruce and Kim.

Just as Petra grew up on the programme so did the pups.

At first they were perfectly easy to control – amongst all the cameras and the complicated electrical equipment and scenery. But when they were thirteen days old, their eyes opened, and then they wanted to explore everywhere and everything. Their huge wicker basket was quite inadequate and we had to think of all kinds of ways in which to barricade them into one place. And we were always having roll calls to make sure none of them was missing.

Petra was a marvellous mother. We'd noticed when she was expecting the pups how she'd become calmer and less highly strung, and

Patch meets Honey, Blue Peter's first Guide Dog for the Blind.

producing a family of eight seemed to have a beneficial effect on her.

She was particularly long suffering with visitors and all the staff working in the studios. When word got round that the pups were in

Studio D each week, Blue Peter seemed to have double the number of engineers and electricians working on it. There'd be a good sprinkling of nurses from the BBC's Surgery, Canteen helpers, Commissionaires and receptionists, too. And considering how possessive many bitches are with their litters, Petra was amazingly relaxed. Maybe her three years in the studios had helped her get used to having plenty of people around, but even so, her acceptance of all the extra puppy-watchers was exceptional.

The pups were all highly photogenic and were obviously great scene-stealers. They made very loud off-stage effects, too. It wasn't easy for Val and Chris to concentrate on serious documentary items, like the story of Captain Carlsen and the Flying Enterprise, or the History of the Fire Brigade, or the development of the American Railways, with eight noisy puppies yapping on the far side of the studio.

But the very fact that the pups *were* so photogenic meant that children who hadn't been particularly interested in dogs were actually writing for information on how to look after a puppy. We'd always stressed that owning any kind of animal meant a great deal of hard work, and hoped very much that seeing the extra work *our* litter caused would make the point.

Soon the pups were learning to eat solid food, instead of just feeding from Petra. By the time they were 5 weeks old, the pups were completely weaned. They didn't need Petra's milk any more – but they still tried to take some and like all bitches with a young litter, Petra became fed up and would chase them off. She started teaching the pups to become independant, and encouraged them to play and race around and have wrestling matches.

Housetraining a big litter is difficult. We covered large areas of the studio floor with newspaper. Not only for reasons of hygiene. Like many other programmes, Blue Peter has always had its studio floor painted – to hide the rather dreary brown linoleum surface. But because the studios are in constant use by many different programmes, the floor paint is soluble and dissolves easily and quickly when it is wet. The surface then becomes like ice and highly dangerous if walked on. If our pups didn't use their newspaper, we were likely to end the day with half the camera crew with broken ankles!

In the end, we built a large wooden pen with steep sides, to try and keep the pups in one place. This became tricky as they grew older, but we were lucky in having a very fine dry autumn, and after they were 3 weeks old, the pups were able to spend most days out of doors. We put a roomy kennel lined with clean straw outside so that they could rest when they were tired of playing.

It's hardly ever possible to keep a whole litter of puppies and we knew we could never end up with nine dogs permanently on the programme. Judging by our postbag, this thought had occurred to Blue Peter viewers, too! It seemed to us that every child in Britain wanted one of the puppies, and wrote pleading to be given one. The letters all contained promises of excellent homes, but we knew that, apart from the fact we'd have to make a personal check on whether or not the homes really *could* cope with a puppy, it would be dreadfully unfair to single out eight of the offers for preferential treatment.

In the end we hit on a solution. We decided not to give the pups away to individual viewers, but to organisations where they'd give pleasure to a lot of people, or to homes where they'd have useful lives as working dogs.

It's not wise to take puppies away from their mothers before they're 8 weeks old and we started to say goodbye to ours when they were 10 weeks.

Candy was the first to go. As she was lively and friendly we thought she'd fit in well with a home with plenty of people around, so we gave her to a Children's Home to be shared by children who would otherwise have no pets. At the British Rail Children's Home at Woking Grange, Andrew Hedges was chosen to look after Candy.

PATCH
ROVER
REX
PETER

CANDY
KIM
PRINCE
BRUCE

Rex and Bruce want to be farm dogs.

Peter and Kim were also given to Children's Homes; while Rex and Bruce went to be farm dogs. They were steady and reliable and we thought they would train easily as sheep and cattle dogs. They were to be family dogs, too, and live indoors with the farmers – not kept outside as kennel dogs.

Rex

Prince

Prince arriving at Salvation Eventide Home.

Prince, who was the smallest of the litter, was a quiet, gentle puppy, so we gave him to an Old People's Home. The Matron of the Salvation Eventide Home near Marlow promised to train him, and she did this so well that Prince was able to spend a lot of time with the old people – to whom he gave a great deal of pleasure.

Prince meets the residents.

Bruce

Kim

Kim and Peter join Children's Homes, too – like their sister, Candy.

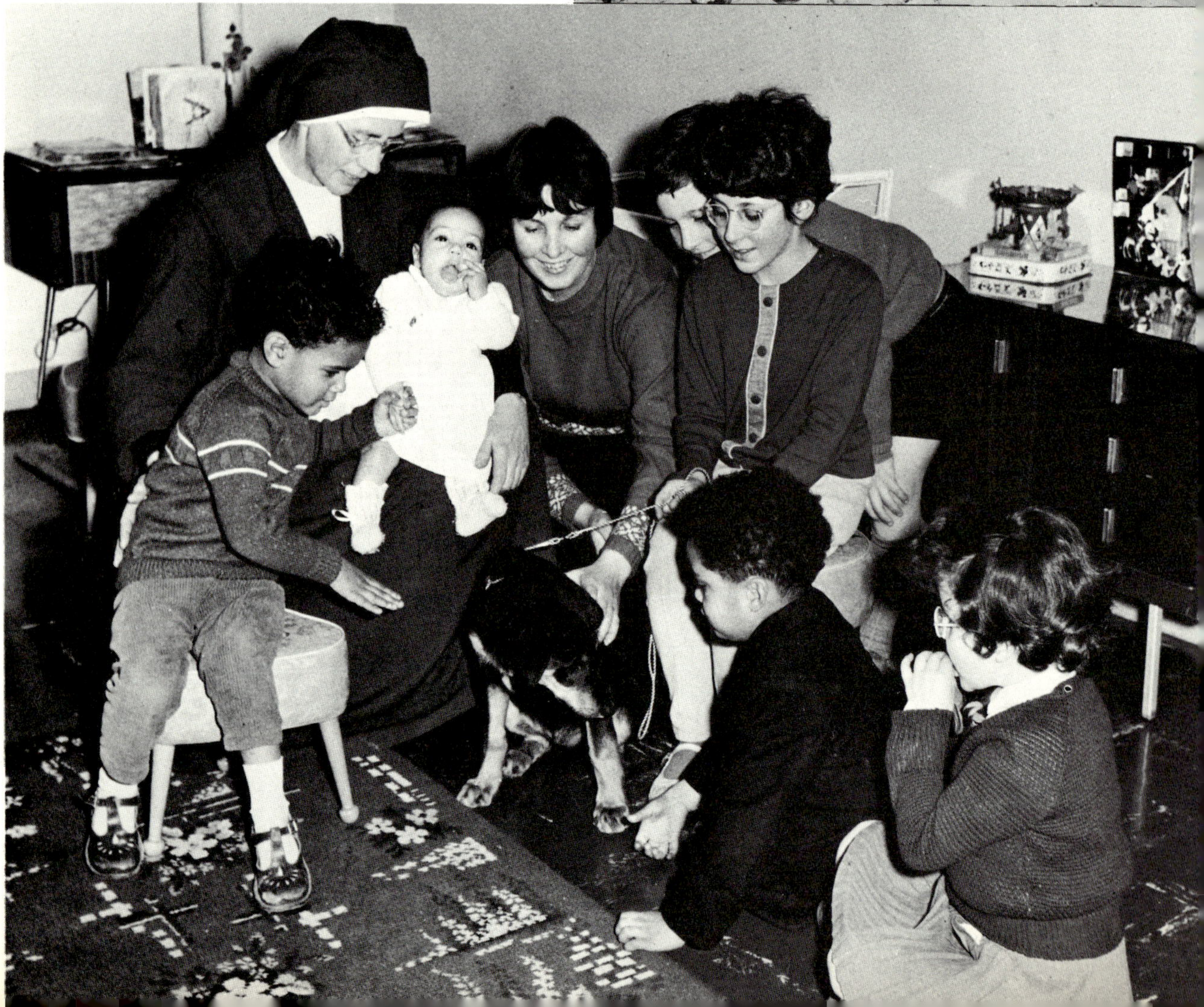

Candy

Rover

Rover was by far the biggest of the puppies. He was so lively and boisterous we thought he'd make a splendid Regimental Mascot. On 30 November 1965 Valerie and Chris – accompanied by Blue Peter film cameras – drove to the Parade Ground of the Junior Leaders' Regiment of the Royal Engineers at Dover. To the rousing tune of the Regimental March, they presented Rover to Sergeant Roy Brooks who was to be his new master.

Even though we knew they'd gone to excellent homes, it was hard parting with the puppies. In the end, we decided to keep one of them, and we chose Patch: Patch, who was to begin his career as Blue Peter's second dog – with the programme's other new boy – John Noakes!

Peter

Patch

Enter John Noakes

Right from the beginning Patch was a nutcase, and by some quirk of fate he became the firm friend of another nutcase, John Noakes.

Some people say that dogs grow like their masters, and others that people get to look like their dogs, but John and Patch bore an uncanny resemblance to each other, both in looks and temperament, from the word go.

"I was a new boy anxious to make good," said John, "and the first challenge they gave me was a dog with a mind of its own. I couldn't remember my words, and Patch wasn't very good at sit and stay, but somehow, we seemed to get by."

Petra and Chris were the good, responsible ones who looked on the antics of John and Patch with a kind of benign tolerance; but Petra was more devoted to Patch than to anybody. They were always delighted to see one another every Monday and Thursday morning when they came to the studio. Throughout the day they played stupid puppy-ish games which used to drive the Floor Manager to distraction. By the time the programme was on the air at five o'clock, they would sink exhausted to the ground and spend the next 25 minutes in a lifeless stupor.

The moment the closing music started they would spring back to life for the next round of neck biting and rolling over.

Just before the summer break in 1967, Christopher Trace told us that he wanted to move to Spain so that he could write a book; so Chris, who had presented the very first Blue Peter on 16 October 1958, left the programme and Petra went to live with Jason in the country. They were looked after by Sylvia Scott, who was Bridget Scott's mother. So in the autumn of 1967 Blue Peter was presented by Val, John, Petra, Patch, Jason and, for a short time, by a green Amazonian parrot called Joey.

Four generations

Petra's grand-puppies were a surprise to us all. They were born to Candy, the only bitch in Petra's litter. Candy, you remember, had gone to the British Rail Children's Home at Woking Grange where she was being looked after by Andrew Hedges, but neither Andrew nor the rest of the children had any idea who the father was. It's not a good thing to let a bitch out to mate indescriminately, but accidents can happen even in the best of families.

Brandy, Dandy and Mandy were born on 22 November 1966. They all had smooth coats, large floppy ears and long tails, and they were all black and tan, except for Brandy who was brown all over. Dandy was the heaviest and was very extrovert and boisterous. Brandy was the quiet one, and Mandy the most mischievous of the three. She looked exactly like Petra when she was born, but although her markings stayed the same she grew floppy ears

Petra and her grand-daughter Mandy and Mandy's puppies, Zebedee and Zabadak.

and only made half the size of her mother.

But it was Mandy who was to continue the dynasty, because on 16 October 1967 Petra's great-grand puppies, Zebedee and Zabadak, were born.

They were both black and white fluffy dogs and didn't look like their grandmother at all. Unfortunately, however, they inherited some of the wilder characteristics of great-uncle Patch. At 3 months old, working as a brace, they managed to tear a newly washed sheet from the line, which they buried, presumably thinking it might come in for another time. The following month they broke into a graveyard by digging a hole under the fence, absconded with a wreath from one of the graves, and chewed it to bits on the lawn. Not a very good beginning, but we were told later that they improved when they got older.

Petra, Candy and Mandy.

Family Tree

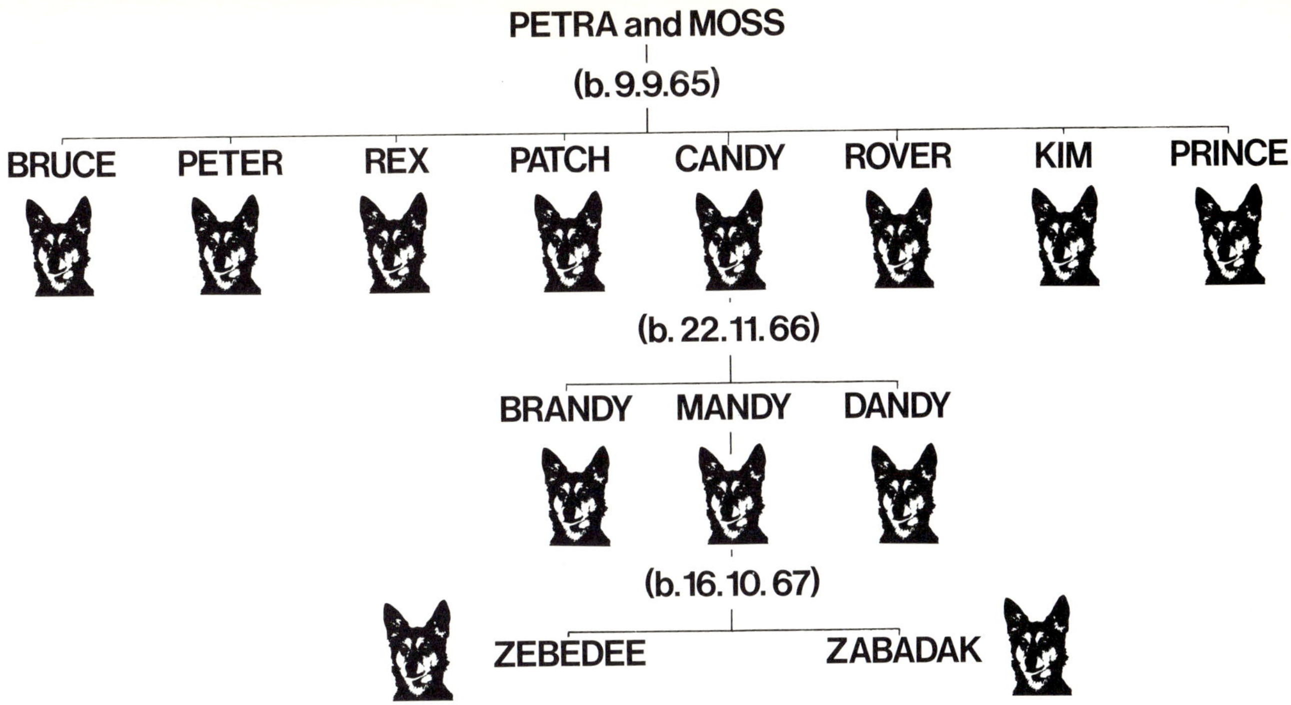

Zabadak.

Three generations.

Peter and Petra

The 16th November 1967 was the best day in Petra's life, because that was when Peter Purves joined Blue Peter. They seemed to take to each other from the very beginning.

Petra always seemed to find a place next to Peter when he was in the studio, and when the whole unit was out on location Petra always fell in behind Peter as if it was the natural thing for her to do.

One of Petra's greatest treats was going out with Peter and Grahame Dangerfield on what we call a "nature walk". Grahame has a wild-life breeding centre where he receives any animal which has been injured. If he can he will cure it, breed from it, and if it is well enough to fend for itself, release it again into the wild.

It was on one of these expeditions to release a kestrel that Petra made her great natural history discovery. She seemed to be showing a great deal of interest in something in the corner of a meadow. She was lying flat on the ground without moving – and refused to come away no matter how much Peter whistled and called. Peter and Grahame approached carefully; Petra still didn't move a muscle. Then Grahame bent down, brushed aside a tuft of grass and revealed a small, terrified baby hare. "Extraordinary thing," he said. "Any other dog I know would have grabbed this little fella by the neck."

Before very long, Peter took Petra to live with his family near Wandsworth Common in South London. She was 5 years old then, and it gave her a new lease of life. A cynical journalist once asked us what happened to the dogs in between the programmes. "They go back home with John and Peter," we told him. The following day he made a surprise call on Peter hoping that he would find that Petra wasn't there, and "reveal all." Instead he found that Peter was out but Petra was at home. It so happened that the journalist was wearing navy blue trousers. Now Petra has never liked men in navy blue trousers since the day she was frightened by a raucous trombone player in the Romford drum and trumpet Corps. Petra gave a low growl and bared her gums: it was lucky for the journalist that Petra had lost all her front teeth.

"It's a good job it wasn't Patch," said John, when Peter told him the story. "He'd have eaten him."

Petra had been well trained and could do all the simple, necessary things – like walking to heel and "sit and stay." But Peter was quick to recognise Petra's intelligence, and her real enjoyment in tackling something difficult. With Peter's patience – and Petra's keeness to please him – they were able to do really challenging exercises, often reaching championship standard. In distance control Peter was able to command Petra to "sit," "lie down," "stand" and "come" when they were 200 yards apart.

Whilst Peter and Petra were together, Peter puppy-walked two guide dogs for the blind, Cindy and Buttons. Puppy-walking takes up an enormous amount of time and energy, because to train any dog you have to win its confidence and affection. It says a great deal for Peter's tact and for Petra's unjealous understanding that she never at any time behaved as if her nose was put out by the presence of those great gambolling Labradors.

Peter's only worry was the enormous responsibility of looking after a dog who had been a star long before he'd started on Blue Peter. Every time he took her for a walk he was terrified in case she got run over.

One misty October evening he was out with Petra on Wandsworth Common, when she

suddenly disappeared. Peter whistled and called until he was hoarse, but there was no sign of Petra. By this time it was dark, and he trudged back home with a sinking heart.

"Most people would have wondered how to explain the situation to their own family," said Peter. "But I had visions of having to go on television and tell eight million people that *I* had lost *their* dog."

He needn't have worried. Petra had got tired of looking for Peter, and had decided to go and wait for him at home!

Petra and Daniel

On 30 December 1968 another new boy joined Blue Peter: Daniel Simon Scott, aged 14 weeks, 2 days. Daniel was the brother of Bridget Scott who first suggested that Jason came on the programme. He was to be the programme's first-ever baby, and the idea was to follow his progress for the first fifteen months of his life.

We wanted to show not only how human babies grew up and developed, but how they differed from animal babies; and we decided the items with Daniel would be far more interesting if John and Peter looked after him rather than Val.

Their reaction couldn't have been more different. John, as usual, took this new development completely in his stride; during rehearsals, he seemed to regard Daniel as a fellow sufferer when he forgot his words or the order in which he had to put Daniel's clothes on. Peter, on the other hand, was not at all happy, particularly when asked to demonstrate things like nappy changing or bottle feeding. When Peter was growing up in the North of England, baby care was strictly for the girls! But in spite of the behind-the-scenes problems, the items with Daniel were a great success, and because John and Peter were so closely involved, so of course, were Patch and Petra.

By this time Petra was 6 years old. She was devoted to Peter, and might well have been jealous of the attention he gave to Daniel, not only in the studio, but during the numerous film sequences. But Petra surprised all of us by taking to Daniel right from the start.

For such a highly-strung dog this was rather remarkable. But she proved so reliable and gentle with the baby that we had no fears at all about the two of them being together during the Daniel items. Just like any ordinary family dog, Petra was around when Daniel was bathed, dressed and fed, and she went on all the walks and outings, too.

It was almost as though Petra regarded Daniel as an overgrown puppy. She let him pull her tail and poke his tiny fists into her face without the slightest sign of bad temper. Patch, however, was rather less reliable and John had to keep a wary eye on him as he was prone to give unexpected nips.

When Daniel stopped being a baby, his television appearances ended too – the last thing we wanted was for him to become a male Shirley Temple.

We knew Daniel was perfectly safe with John and Peter and was in no danger from any of the technical equipment. His mother sat only a few feet away from him – just out of vision of the cameras – and we always had a "stand-by" item ready, in case Daniel showed any signs of

not wanting to join in.

Petra played a big part in the smooth running of the items. Her presence made them like any other Blue Peter project. It was much more relaxing to have her there – and that helped enormously, for babies are amazingly quick to react to any undercurrents of tension.

Of course, at the time, we took it all for granted. But looking back, we were very lucky Petra reacted so well. It's asking a great deal of any dog to expect good behaviour all the time – but on a "live" TV programme that's the demand that is made. Petra rarely let us down!

Bathing the dogs

Beyond a shadow of a doubt, Petra's most unfavourite day was when she and Patch had their annual bath in the studio. She didn't hate it quite as much as Jason did, but Jason's bath was a once in a lifetime disaster that was never to be repeated.

Patch always did the obvious things like shaking himself all over John, but Petra felt the heavy weight of responsibility and tried her best to get it right.

The thing that confused her the most was being bathed "dry" during all the rehearsals. We never used water until we were on the air, because the dogs would have had three or four baths during the course of the day and might well have caught pneumonia. Petra didn't mind the "dry" baths at all, although she probably thought that being lifted in and out of an empty bath was a little unnecessary. But when transmission came and jugs of real water were poured over her, and real soap was rubbed in, she couldn't believe it – it was like a betrayal. She would sit in the bath whilst bucket after bucket of water was poured over her without moving an inch, only occasionally did she cast a disdainful glance at Peter. "Traitor," she thought.

But like all other dogs, once it was all over and she was dry again she almost looked as though she felt it had been worthwhile.

Well, anyway, it was better than being wet.

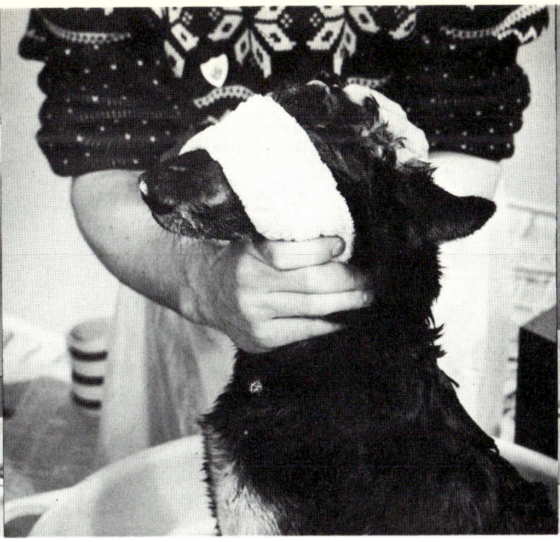

MOON

Death of Patch

On 18 May 1971 David Brown, one of the Blue Peter directors, made an idyllic film about the waterways of Britain at the turn of the century. Val, John and Peter were all dressed in the costume of the period, and they sailed in a beautiful narrow boat pulled by dappled-grey dray horses along the Grand Union Canal. Petra and Patch loved making this particular film. The boat was so long and narrow that they were able to run along its whole length, and the banks were never further than a dog's jump away.

What we didn't know at the time was that it was going to be Patch's last film.

He was such a jolly dog, and he had always been so fit that no one had ever had a moment's anxiety about him in all the years he had been on the programme.

The next day John thought Patch was a bit mopish and off colour, but he wasn't particu-

larly worried. But the following day he seemed worse. John sent for the vet, who thought from the symptoms that Patch had picked up some kind of poison. By the end of the week he was dead. The autopsy revealed that it had not been poison but a rare disease called E Coli Septicaemia.

John for all his jokes and his clowning is a very private person. Not many people really know what goes on in his mind. Off the screen he always tried to give the impression that Patch was just another responsibility we had lumbered him with, but you didn't have to be a great psycho-analyst to know that there was a really close relationship between John and Patch.

The day after Patch died there were thousands of letters from viewers all over Britain saying how sorry they were, and we included some of them in the programme. During the rehearsals, whilst John was reading out some of these letters, that tough little Yorkshireman – who is afraid of nothing and nobody – suddenly stopped. He couldn't see the writing through his tears.

One knows even less of what goes on in a dog's mind. Petra was definitely not herself for a week or so after Patch had died. She had lost a friend whose company she had enjoyed since the day he was born.

Arrival of Shep

At first John couldn't contemplate the idea of having another dog. He felt he had owed a lot to Patch, because in a way it was Patch who helped John to find his own role on Blue Peter. However, when he came back from the summer filming trip to Scandinavia, he looked somehow "undressed" without a dog at his heels.

John has always had a great admiration for

working dogs. He admires professional skills, and is attracted by people who are able to do something brilliantly, whether it's Yehudi Menuhin playing the violin or Reg Dosell, the steeplejack, climbing Nelson's Column. In the animal world, a Border Collie working sheep and responding to commands from a shepherd who may be a clear two miles away is the height of professional achievement. It fired John's imagination so much that he decided to have a Border Collie of his own.

Shep arrived on 10 September 1971. He was 8 weeks old, fluffy, floppy eared and bursting with curiosity. He had a cat-like fascination for everything that moved. Any moving object – a balloon, a football, a model train – was a challenge which had to be overtaken and brought back to the leader.

Petra was approaching her ninth birthday when Shep arrived. Quite old in dog years, and she was beginning to look a little grey round the muzzle. She might have been forgiven if she had been a bit grumpy with the boisterous newcomer taking over *her* studio. But not a bit of it. Petra seemed to think that Shep was there for her own personal pleasure; and the endless puppyish games reminiscent of the old days with Patch began to drive everybody round the bend again.

Petra was never a jealous dog, and the confidence that Peter had given her made her so sure of her own position that she never felt threatened. Dog and cats and parrots came and went, but Petra was the senior, the original Blue Peter dog; and she seemed to know it.

Famous faces

No dog has ever, in the history of dogs, sat at the feet of so many of the great. It is possible that Dash, Queen Victoria's dog, and the present Queen's corgis may have had the edge on her as far as Royal personages are concerned, but when it came to famous people, Petra could lick them all.

Not that Petra has been ignored by the Royal Family. Princess Anne made a great fuss of her when she came to the Blue Peter studio to show her wildlife photographs after "Blue Peter Royal Safari": "I can remember seeing you as a puppy when I was a girl at school," she said. And long before that, Princess Anne's younger brothers, Prince Andrew and Prince Edward, had come to the studio on a private visit as a half-term treat with their cousins Viscount Linley and Lady Sarah Armstrong Jones.

Petra's early experiences with the trombone player in the Romford Drum and Trumpet Band certainly prejudiced her against musicians en masse, particularly if they were wearing dark blue trousers; but she was always very pleasant with soloists. Yehudi Menuhin, the

Left: Prince Edward visiting the Blue Peter studio.

Below: Petra rehearsing with Princess Anne.

great violinist, played especially for her, and she was very attached to James Galway, the brilliant Irish flautist. Musicians who moved about, however, like Roy Castle playing the spoons and the slate xylophone, were a greater hit with Shep, who can't wait to get into everybody's act. It was the quieter ones who came to talk that were Petra's favourites.

Not that she was at all highbrow. Ringo Starr and David Cassidy were made every bit as welcome as Dame Margot Fonteyn and Yehudi Menuhin. Although we must confess that she did bite a hole in the Hollies' bass guitar player's trousers. But they *were* navy blue trousers, and he was jumping up and down and playing rather loudly at the time.

That was the only occasion that Petra showed any aggression to a visitor. In fact, she was able to put people at their ease more quickly than any courtier or public relations officer. Even the great, perhaps particularly the great, are often shy, ill at ease or nervous when they come to be interviewed on television. They are sometimes suspicious and worried in case they might be asked an embarrassing question that would be difficult for them to answer. The studio staff, the producer and the presenters always go to a lot of trouble to help visitors to relax, but nine times out of ten it was the soft brown muzzle being placed quietly in their laps that made them feel they were in a friendly world.

You can never be certain how a younger person is going to behave in the studio. Some are scared out of their wits and reduced to "yes" and "no" answers, or even just nods and shakes, whilst others feel tremendously at home, and given the opportunity would talk all the way from "Hello there" – to – "We'll be back on Thursday."

Garry Fridd, the Yorkshire boy who found a £10,000 Mediaeval sword in a stream, fell into neither category. He was quietly confident without being at all big-headed or pushy. Petra gave him a wag of approval when he gave her a pat on the head after he had been introduced to Peter. Then he sat on the bench with Peter and Petra and told his amazing story with superb clarity.

Petra had been present for moments of history and for moments of tragedy. She was there when the British Everest Expedition came to the studio in 1975 before they set off for the Himalayas; and she was patted by Expedition Leader Chris Bonington, and mountaineers Doug Scott and Dougal Haston. The Expedition cameraman, Mick Burke, she already knew, because he had worked on several Blue Peter films in the past. It was Mick who promised to take the Blue Peter Flag to plant on the summit of Everest. She was there when the triumphant but saddened party returned having conquered the South West face, but had had to leave behind their comrade Mick, who had died in the attempt to be the first man to shoot moving pictures from the summit of the world.

Petra took part in the very first Blue Peter Appeal in 1963, and was photographed with Chris and Val on top of the huge pile of parcels of toys for deprived children. Since then she has seen three guide dogs for the blind puppy-walked and trained. There have been Hospital Trucks and Emergency Doctors' cars for war-torn Nigeria, Hot Dinner Vans for the elderly

Top left: Peter and Petra with Gary Fridd and his £10,000 sword.

Top right: Petra and a Blue Peter Hospital Truck.

Bottom: Petra with the men who conquered the south-west face of Everest.

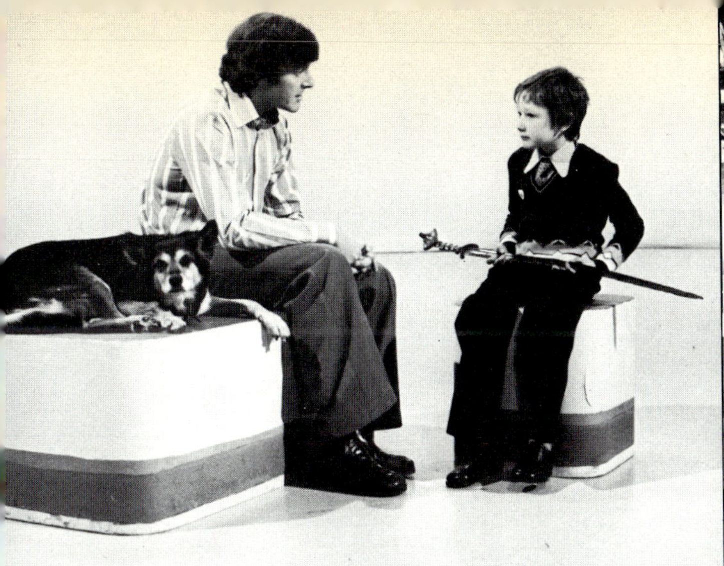

BLUE PETE
HOSPITAL
TRUCK

and Holiday Caravans for poor children. A dormitory for an African Boys School, Houses for the Homeless and aid for war orphans. Petra went to the Depot every year and climbed over mountains of tin foil, cotton waste, scrap metal and postage stamps. As a result of one appeal alone, it is a plain fact that during Petra's lifetime 264 people who would have drowned are alive today because of four Inshore Life Boats supplied by Blue Peter viewers.

Perhaps Petra's greatest honour was when the famous wild-life sculptor William Timym asked us if he could make a statue of her. After making several drawings "Tim" asked if Petra would come to his studio to pose whilst he made a clay model from which the final bronze would be cast. She and Peter went day after day, Petra sitting patiently as ever, while Peter gave her encouragement, and under Tim's hands the figure in clay began to emerge.

The result was a truly beautiful bronze statue. We were very proud of it at the time and gave it a place of honour in the Blue Peter office, but we didn't realise then how much it would mean to us, and to millions of viewers in only a few years' time.

Death of Jason

On 16 January 1976 Jason, our Siamese cat, caught a chill and four days later he died of kidney failure. He was nearly twelve years old.

It would be untrue to say that Petra mourned him deeply, but they had learned to live with each other over the years. Perhaps she missed having no one to pointedly ignore any more! Many people were saddened by Jason's death, including the Oxford University Union, who sent us a letter saying that the Union stood in silence for two minutes, after they had passed the resolution, "This house regrets the passing of Jason the Blue Peter Cat."

Perhaps they were also mourning the passing of their own childhood because most of the undergraduates would have been eight or nine years old when Jason first appeared on Blue Peter.

Somehow, Blue Peter didn't seem the same without a cat, and on 19 February we introduced our new twins, Jack and Jill, two Silver Spotted Tabbies. They'd been bred by an old friend of the programme's, Edith Menezes. Considering that Petra was now thirteen years old, she displayed remarkable tolerance towards the twins. They were two of the most lively and mischievous kittens imaginable, and there were many occasions during Blue Peter's "live" transmissions when we held our breaths and hoped that Petra's good nature wouldn't be stretched to its limit. But there were no ugly scenes; just the odd low warning growl. A veteran of over a thousand programmes wasn't going to be driven from *her* seat in the studio by two tiresome tabbies!

Birthdays

"There is a man named Peter
Who has a dog called Petra
And they both appear on the BBC
On a programme called Blue Peter.
On Sunday Petra is eleven
And should live for another seven."
(*Blue Peter Viewer: November* 1973)

Very few human beings, let alone animals, can have received a fraction of the post bag that regularly reached the Blue Peter office early each November. Petra's birthday was always celebrated on the nearest Monday or Thursday to 4 November, and by tradition, every single card was displayed in the studio. We must have got through more rolls of double-sided sticky tape on the birthdays than on any other days of the year. Television studios are large, draughty places, and it wasn't enough for our designer to arrange an artistic display – each card had to be firmly glued in place. After the afternoon post – only a couple of hours before Blue Peter's "live" transmission – the whole office would descend on the studio to give the hard pressed designer a hand. So much thought and loving care had gone into the cards, we wanted each one to be displayed to its best advantage.

Mostly the cards were home made, and showed great ingenuity: like Happy Birthday spelt out in cardboard cut-out bones and strung together as a mobile, or cartoons showing Petra in hair-raising situations in the studio or in front of our film cameras, and once a whole birthday newspaper called *The Dog Times*, full of doggy news like the football results:
"Queen's Bark Rangers beat Leeds United 3-1."
"Wolves beat Barking 2-nil."

On her thirteenth birthday one viewer sent Petra the whole story of her birthday in words and pictures. It started at 10.00 a.m. with Petra saying, "I think I'll take another hour in bed," and jumped to twelve o'clock when it was time to go to the studio and, "The Manageress of Blue Peter came with at least 70 letters and 14 parcels for her." Later in the day, the card read, "Soon the programme began and the studio was full of cards, and of course Petra was

13 years old – but she did not know it – because she was asleep!" Val, John, Peter and Lesley would always read out some of the rhymes and jokes, and then there'd be the agonising moments just before transmission, when the programme was too long and cuts had to be made. No one wanted to drop any of the cards they were showing or reading out – particularly the funny ones.

One year, we created our own not-so-funny situation when Petra didn't have her slice of birthday cake – at least not whilst the programme was being televised.

The "cake" was always ordinary dog food covered with meaty flavoured margerine that looked like icing sugar. With a cake frill and lighted candles, the cakes could have been mouthwatering creations from a smart confectioner. But they only had to be left under the fiercely hot studio lights for a few minutes for the pungent aroma of chunky morsels to pervade the air – much to the delight of the dogs and Jason. As the human members of the team would have found the smell of dog-cake unbearable for a whole afternoon's rehearsals, we always had the real cake stored in a refrigerator and used a dummy for rehearsing things like lighting the candles and the actual cutting – which had to be at exactly the right angle for the cameras.

One year, the Assistant Floor Manager completely forgot the real cake until the red studio lights were flashing their warning that there were only seconds to go before Blue Peter was "ON AIR." The result was a frozen, rock-hard cake which defied the united attempts of John, Peter and Lesley to cut it. Chips of iced morsels flew in all directions, while faces reddened and excuses were muttered. The animals alone remained calm and dignified. The frozen cake smelled hygienically of nothing – so they didn't know what they were missing!

Petra's fourteenth birthday was a very moving occasion. We all knew her health was failing, and we all felt that it would probably be the last one with Petra as a regular member of the team. Because of that, we all made a special effort to see the display of cards was the best-ever, and because Petra was becoming increasingly rheumaticy in her back legs, we gave her a warm brown-and-yellow checked blanket as her present from the programme with her name stitched on one corner. It was an appropriate present, but a sad one. During the next nine months, Petra used the blanket more and more as she became less mobile, and we began to realise she couldn't carry on.

Petra retires

The difficult thing about making the decision to retire Petra was that she was in no pain.

Lying in her favourite place at Pete's feet by the studio seats, or sitting up with him on the padded cushions, Petra looked alert and happy. There were a lot of grey hairs, she no longer chased Shep in and out of the shelves, and she had very few teeth, but her ears remained pricked and, although she was extremely deaf, she followed Peter's movements like a hawk.

But the fact was that Petra had rheumatism in her back legs, her sight was failing, and to crown it all, she had been diagnosed as diabetic.

We made this discovery when Petra was twelve. She'd gone to the vet, as she'd seemed off colour, but the resulting diagnosis was the last thing we'd expected. It meant she had to be given a lot of extra care and attention – although the vet said he saw no reason why Petra shouldn't carry on in the studio, providing she took life gently, was given her medicines regularly and kept on a fairly strict diet.

For Peter to combine this extra care with his heavy filming schedules was obviously going to be impossible. Very reluctantly, he agreed to hand Petra over to Edith, who'd volunteered to look after her.

It was a wrench for Peter, but far better for Petra than being left for hours on her own, while he was away filming. And Edith was a friend, not a complete stranger. Her huge garden made a marvellous playground for Petra who still much preferred being out of doors.

We'd made no secret of the fact Petra was diabetic and, strangely enough, the news seemed to give children who also suffered from diabetes a great deal of encouragement. This letter from a $10\frac{1}{2}$-year-old boy was typical of the ones we received:

> Dear Blue Peter,
>
> I have just found out that Petra has diabetis. I found out that I had it two weeks ago and I had to go into hospital. I have one Jab of insulin in the morning. Could you please tell me does Petra have a Jab take pills or is she just on a special diet?

In May 1977 a 6-year-old viewer from Redcar wrote:

> Dear Petra
>
> My name is Nicholas Wighton and I am six years old. I only heard the other day that you are diabetic I am diabetic as well as you and on May 29th my mummy is having a jubilee party just for diabetic children so that we dont feel left out of the celebrations I would like you to come to my party if it is possible. My mummy will give youre injection
>
> Lots of love
>
> Nicholas

We showed the letter to Edith and asked if she felt able to drive to Redcar in Cleveland and back. To our delight she said, "Yes." On 29 May Edith and her friend Betty started off on their 500 mile round trip with Petra and – as an added bonus for the Jubilee Party – Jack and Jill.

It was a huge success. The local paper, the *Evening Gazette*, was there to take photographs, the local Council chipped in with Jubilee flags and kindly shopkeepers sent free milk and

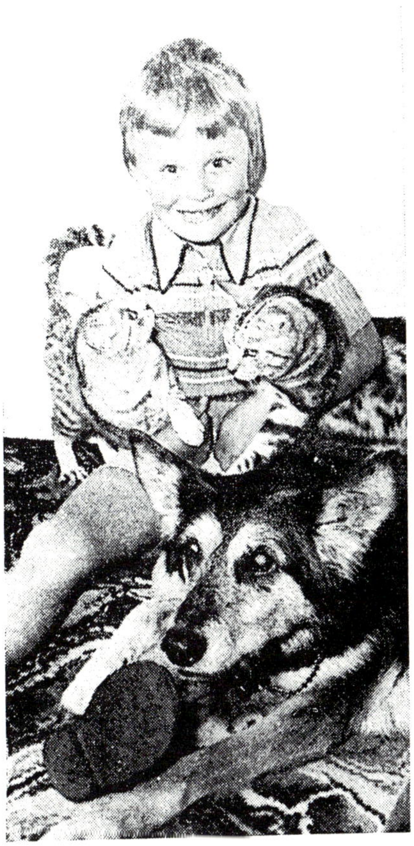

Blue Peter trio make his day

A SIX-YEAR-OLD BOY who needs two injections a day to live had the icing on the cake at his party yesterday.

And it was put there by the BBC and Langbaurgh Council. For they helped Nicholas Wighton to celebrate his birthday and the Queen's Jubilee at a party thrown for fellow diabetics at his home in Sycamore Road, Redcar.

What made the occasion extra special was the guests of honour—Petra, the alsatian, and his feline friends Jack and Jill from "Blue Peter" with whom the happy birthday boy is pictured.

The BBC had been so touched by the party invitation Nicholas sent out to Petra—also a diabetic—that it arranged for all three resident animals on Blue Peter to travel to Teesside with Mrs. Edith Menezes, their keeper.

Langbaurgh's parks department decided the occasion warranted a splash of colour and sent workers round to put out the flags at Nicholas' home.

Jubilee joy

It all went down a treat with 30 children from Teesside Dabetic Association who would otherwise have missed out on jubilee street fun.

"None of the children could go to a street party because they needed special diets at specific times," said Nicholas' mum, Mrs. Susan Wighton.

Local shopkeepers and deliverymen also chipped in with free milk and diabetic foods.

diabetic foods. For Nicholas and his friends it was the party of a lifetime; for us it was a poignant reminder that, old and ill as she was, Petra still had a very special place in the hearts of even the youngest viewers.

But much as we hated the idea of doing Blue Peter without Petra, by June 1977 we knew it was becoming increasingly unfair to subject her to the upheaval of her twice weekly studio appearances.

The slippery studio floor was a difficult walking surface for her. She began to skid and sprawl so much that in the end Peter or Edith or our Floor Manager, Derek Kibble, carried her to and from her place in front of the cameras.

Petra was much steadier on grass, and was always quite lively when we were recording our Blue Peter garden items with Percy Thrower, or out at the front of Television Centre pruning our silver birch, the Blue Peter Tree for the Year Two Thousand. Even so, she wasn't nearly as mobile as she'd been even a few months before, and we decided that we'd have to announce her retirement on our last programme before the 1977 summer break.

Because we wanted to break the news gently, we threw out a hint of what was to happen on the programme *before* the retirement announcement date. John, Pete and Lesley asked viewers to be sure to watch on 30 June, as there was to be "some important news" about Petra. By the following post we received these agonised appeals:

To All at "Blue Peter"
PLEASE
PLEASE
DO NOT HAVE "PETRA"
PUT TO Sleep because
She is old we love her
You Are going to tell us
Something horrible on Thursday
We know you are
Please Please Do not
take her lovely Life
We love her.

Dear Lesley, John, Peter, and Miss Baxter,
My Aunty is helping me write this letter,
We have just heard Lesley say she is
going to tell us Something about "Petra"
on Thursday, I hope it is nothing
about her being too old to be
wanted any more, it has made my
friend Joan and me very sad we
cried Please Dont have "Petra"
Put to sleep everyone Loves her
we have all got to get old
I know her eye sight is bad, our
doggie went blind we still kept her
until she died ^16yrs we all loved her so,
and she was bad on her legs like
"Petra", Please Keep her she looks
so fragile, we are all very
sad to-night I cant stop
thinking about what Lesley said
Love from
Janet Blake x

Those two letters made us even more certain that to avoid millions more children being deeply upset, we'd have to word the retirement announcement very very carefully indeed.

This is an exact transcript of what Peter said:

"We said that today we'd be making a very important announcement about Petra – and this is it. Next November Petra will be 15 years old. That's a great age for a dog – some people would say it's equivalent to being a hundred and five for a human! She's not in any pain, but she *is* a very old lady, and as well as being diabetic, she's rather deaf and her back legs are getting weak, and it's difficult for her to walk about on the slippery studio floor. So we think the kindest thing to do is to let her retire and save her the upheaval of travelling backwards and forwards to the studio twice a week. I think she's going to have a very happy retirement, because she'll be staying with Jack and Jill, who are looked after by a friend of ours. So we'll be keeping closely in touch with her.

"The people who were 5 years old when Petra made her very first appearance on Blue Peter are nearly 20 years old now! And when we did a bit of arithmetic, we worked out that Petra's appeared on no less than 1,192 Blue Peter's – and clocked up the incredible total of 555 *hours* of television. Here's how it all began."

Then followed an eight-and-a-half minute film and videotape biography that covered the whole of Petra's Blue Peter life. It ended with a very beautiful sequence of Petra when she was being sculpted by William Timym. It was a moving occasion, especially for Peter and those of us behind-the-scenes who'd worked with Petra for nearly fifteen years.

The day before, Petra had had her last press call – we'd hoped that news of her retirement in the morning papers would help prepare the way for the news on the programme. Just as in September 1965 when Petra's pups first came to the studio, photographers from the national press and the agencies crowded into the Blue Peter garden at the back of the BBC Television Centre's canteen. It was a warm, sunny day, and we wanted Petra to be photographed where she was happiest – out of doors.

Peter sat with Petra on the grass, while Edith fielded Jack and Jill who were darting amongst the broad beans and roses. In the end we gave up trying to include them in the photographs. Then the photographers asked Peter to hold Petra while they snapped away at her in his arms, and we asked the BBC photographer to take some shots of Petra with Edith, too.

We all ended up fairly hot and sticky – the calmest of the bunch was Petra who gave us a look as though she was thinking "for heaven's sake – not *another* lot of photos." A fair reaction from the most photographed dog in Britain!

Edith with Petra.

Goodbye Petra

Straight after Blue Peter ended on 30 June 1977, John, Peter and Lesley began to prepare and pack for the programme's summer expedition to the world's fifth largest country – Brazil.

Petra set off with Edith and Jack and Jill on her last journey from Television Centre – accompanied by Shep who was also spending the summer with Edith, while John was in South America.

And thousands of Blue Peter viewers sat down to write letters sadly accepting that Petra's retirement *was* the right move. The letters came from all over the country and from viewers of all ages, like 5-year-old Julie who said:

Dear Blue Peter I am very sad for Petra not to be going on tlevishann

I hope she likes it at the farm.

love fom Julie x x x

Seven-year-old Nicola wrote:

Dear Blue Peter,
I am sad that Petra is retiring. I enjoyed the film about her when she was a puppy and I liked her puppys very much.
I hope that Petra has a happy time in the country. She will enjoy herself when Jack and Jill and Shep come to stay.

I am sorry she is too weak to walk on the studio.
I like Blue Peter very much

Love from
Nicola Derryn Watson
Age 7.

We were surprised and touched by the number of teenagers who wrote, like the 16-year-old boy from Nottingham who said:

DEAR ALL,
I MUST WRITE TO EXSPRESS MY SORROW OVER PETRA'S RETIRMENT, ALTHOUGH I AGREE, AFTER READING THE PAPERS & SEEING THE PROGRAM IT IS ONLY FAIR & FITTING THAT SUCH A FINE OLD LADY SHOULD RETIRE TO THE QUITE DURING HER LATER YEARS OF LIFE.
THE LENGTH OF TIME SHE HAS LIVED ONLY UNDERLINES HOW WELL SHE HAS BEEN LOOKED AFTER, I SALOUT TO A GRAND OLD LADY.
WHEN JASON DIED YOU WERE GOOD ENOUGH TO SEND ME A PICTURE COULD I HAVE ONE OF PETRA PLEASE

YOUR FAITHFULLY

P.S I LEFT WORK AT 4.30 INSTEAD OF 5.00 TO SEE THE PROGRAME 30 JUNE AFTER REDING IN THE PAPERS.

There were letters from old age pensioners, shift workers, au pair girls and some of the "children" who first saw Petra on Blue Peter when they were little, who were now watching with children of their own.

Dear John, Lesley, Peter and Petra,

I'm writing to wish Petra a happy retirement

Thank you all for the years of great programmes, I've been a pretty regular watcher since you started. I'm now 24 years old, and watch with the children — I haven't outgrown the best ever childrens programme yet, and have concluded that i won't now.

Congratulations to you all for the super animals you've got, happy (belated) birthday to Shep, and love to Petra - I've had a soft spot for her for a very long time.

With best wishes,
Yours sincerely,
Jane M. Springer (Mrs).

Petra was even considered important enough to impinge on one viewer's honeymoon!

Dear Lesley, Pete and John,

I would just like to say how sorry I am to hear that Petra is going to be retired.

I am 21 years old and was one of those 5 year olds that you mentioned when Petra first joined Blue Peter. Luckily the time I get in from work I am able to watch Blue Peter and still enjoy it very much especially when you have animals on the programme.

Petra is very special to me because in Christmas 1975 I looked after a 5 week old puppy which was abandoned and when it was time to find her a home I couldn't part with her. I gave her a name but decided I didn't like it and so I decided to call her Petra after your dog in hope that she would grow up well behaved and a dog to be proud of - and this she has lived up to like your dog. She also watches Blue Peter with me when I come home from work and she is very keen on Shep!!!

I hope you read my letter, by the time you get back from Rio I will be married and on my honeymoon but we have a television in our room so I shall try and make a point of seeing your programme.

Please keep us up to date on how Petra gets on as she is very special to me - tears came to my eyes when Pete announced on the T.V. Thursday that she was going.

Best wishes for the future and give Petra a pat from me. You all do a wonderful job which brings great enjoyment to a lot of children. Long live Blue Peter.

We had every intention of keeping Blue Peter viewers in touch with Petra. As soon as Peter returned from Brazil, he drove down to

Edith's and we filmed him in the garden with Petra, Shep and Jack and Jill. It was all very simple. Petra lay on her birthday-present rug and Peter stroked her gently and gave her a marrow bone to lick as she watched Shep fool about and the cats doing their usual disappearing act. And although, when we saw the "rushes" – the developed film – before it was cut and edited, Petra seemed to have become much frailer than she was at the beginning of the summer, little did we know that that film was to be the very last one starring Petra – or that the photographs taken on that day would be Petra's very last pictures.

We'd had many conversations with Edith about Petra's state of health and she kept us in touch with regular bulletins from the vet. During the second week of September, just one week before Blue Peter was due to return to the screen after the summer break, Edith rang to say Petra's back legs were practically useless. But she was still in no pain and strong enough to bark.

On Thursday 12 September, Blue Peter was back on the air. During the usual round-up of summer holiday news we said how weak Petra had become and passed on the news from Edith.

On Tuesday night, Edith rang in great distress. Petra was now so weak she couldn't even move to urinate. With this news, our minds were made up. It seemed utterly wrong to keep any animal alive in such a condition, so we asked Edith to take Petra to the vet the following morning, to be put to sleep quickly and painlessly.

A short, tearful telephone call at 10.15 a.m. on Wednesday told us this had been done. Petra had ended her life peacefully aged 14 years, 10 months and 20 days.

The BBC Press Officer put out a telex and, within an hour, news of Petra's death had been read out on the Radio News bulletins – even the Radio 1 pop shows had been interrupted.

The Blue Peter office has some fourteen telephone extensions – for the whole of Wednesday they all seemed to be ringing at once. The calls came from every corner of the country, from newspaper reporters, magazines, local broadcasting stations, from children and from adults.

Even though we knew Petra was enormously popular, we were quite unprepared for the flood of feeling and interest, and for the sympathy and thoughtfulness expressed by the callers. "I've just heard it on the news," said one lady on a long distance line, "I just had to ring and tell you how sorry I am."

We manned the office during the lunch hour, thanked all the people who rang up, sent off dozens of photos to the clamouring picture editors, who all wanted to run Petra stories, and re-wrote the script for Thursday's programme.

After the lunchtime Television News, we were very touched to hear Michael Fish, the Weather Man, pay tribute to Petra, and John Craven also made some moving comments on his Newsround programme. Petra was mentioned on the early evening Television News, too, and just before that, we'd had an anxious taxidermist on the line, hoping he could send a refridgerated van for Petra's body, so that it could be stuffed and put on public display!

Five proprietors of Pets' Cemetaries offered free plots for Petra's grave but, like the taxidermist's offer, there was no question of them being accepted. We'd promised Edith long ago that when Petra died she could be buried in her garden. Edith had even discovered a pale purple rhododendron called Blue Peter, and she was busy tracking one down to plant on the grave.

On Thursday morning Petra hit the headlines like no other dog before or since. She was news in every single national paper from *The Times* to the *Mirror* and the *Sun*. Weeks later, when the cuttings from the provincial papers came in, she seemed to be in each of them too.

We were immensely grateful for all the television and press coverage, because we

by police

Daily Mail, Thursday, September 15

Petra, the pet every child knew is dead

PETRA, the TV dog loved by generations of Blue Peter viewers is dead.

Her owners at the BBC decided that she was too old and ill, and on the advice of a vet she was put to sleep yesterday.

By MARTIN JACKSON
TV Editor

Petra had clocked up more than 550 hours on TV in a remarkable career spanning 15 years.

She had millions of admirers, including Princes Andrew and Edward. And on each birthday up to 100,000 cards and presents would flow into the *Blue Peter* studio.

Loved

Last night Biddy Baxter the programme's editor, said: 'We all loved Petra dearly, but putting her down was the kindest thing to do.

'Her health had deteriorated rapidly since the beginning of the month and she had lost the use of her back legs.

Today Petra will be seen making her 1,193rd and final TV appearance on film made earlier in the summer in Sussex with the *Blue Peter* cats Jack and Jill and Shep, the dog that replaced her on the programme when she retired eight months ago.

Petra caught the imagination of viewers of all ages when she was introduced on TV in 1962 as a six-week-old puppy.

But over the years her appeal went much further.

The mongrel was petted by Princess Anne and appeared with Dame Margot Fonteyn, Yehudi Menuhin, Ringo Starr and David Cassidy.

Petra, with presenter Valerie Singleton in 1962

TV dog Petra dies after 15 years on Blue Peter

WEDNESDAY, SEPTEMBER

...sion dog dies: Petra, who appeared in the BBC television programme, "Blue Peter" for nearly 15 years until retirement in June, died yesterday. She was introduced to the series in 1962 as a television pet for children who live in tower blocks and could not keep animals of their

...that first ... was 15 years ... own right—

...was a dog for ... was still there and were able ... at over Petra's

...deaf and suffer- ... of adults sent

...best wishes by ... that Petra, in ... of care at a ... condition ... her

...fair to bring her to the studio twice a week. "But we promised not to touch and during the ... filmed her in the ... with the ... Jill

...it would be the last film ever made of her. This is going to be one of the saddest pieces of news we've ever given out on Blue Peter.

"Her health deteriorated rapidly since the beginning of September and reluctantly ... make the very ... have her

...Blue Peter in June.

DAILY MIRROR, Thursday, September

Farewell to TV's top dog

By TONY PRATT

PETRA, Britain's best-loved dog and star of the children's T V show Blue Peter, is dead.

The 15-year-old dark brown mongrel, who first appeared on Blue Peter as a six-week-old puppy, was retired last June because of ill-health.

And yesterday the show's editor, Biddy Baxter, said: "Reluctantly we had to make the very hard decision to have Petra put to sleep.

"Her health deteriorated rapidly and she had lost the use of her back legs."

... favourite with millions of children and received 100,000 cards and presents each birthday.

She appeared with royalty and pop stars during her T V career.

Peter Purves, the Blue Peter presenter who looked after Petra at his home for five years, said: "Petra was a smashing dog. She was fast and clever."

Petra's last film — of her in retirement in Sussex — will be shown on today's edition of Blue Peter.

CHILDREN'S FAVOURITE: Blue Peter's Petra

wanted to do everything we could to soften the blow of giving the news of Petra's death on Blue Peter itself.

It was not an easy day in the studio. Even though we'd all been expecting Petra's death, the actual moment of explaining that it had happened brought a lump to all our throats.

We showed the film of Peter going to visit Petra after the Brazil expedition, and Peter went on to say that we liked to remember Petra best as she'd been when she was fit and lively – a real outdoor, sporting dog. And we ran some film of her with Peter and Shep on a very happy outing to the sea.

We'd brought Tim's bronze of Petra to the studio, and Peter put it on the shelves – so that in a sense she'd stay in the studio; and because we'd been so moved by the response we'd had to the news of Petra's death, Peter said that if people sent stamped, addressed envelopes, we'd post back photos of Petra as a remembrance.

Afterwards, Peter said he'd never ever been so nervous on any programme since he joined Blue Peter nine years previously. "It was knowing that whatever happened, I mustn't make a mistake that terrified me," he said. "I was literally shaking all through the programme."

Within one week we'd received over 40,000 requests for Petra's photograph, and two months later, requests were still coming in. After we'd exhausted supplies of all the coloured postcards, we had a black and white photo printed that was particularly special. It was the very last snap ever taken of Petra, and we sent a note explaining this with the photos that went out.

Letters of sympathy are still reaching the Blue Peter office – including many kind offers of replacement puppies, and all sorts of other pets. Some people sent postal orders or cheques to "buy something to cheer Shep up" or for Jack and Jill.

Shep certainly moped for a week or two; there's no doubt he missed Petra even though she'd been inactive during her last year alive.

Other viewers sent donations in remembrance of Petra to be put towards some good cause, or to go towards an animal charity of our choice. About half the letters asked if it would be possible to have a statue erected in Petra's honour, and Tim suggested that he sculpted a new and much larger bronze that could be put up out-of-doors at Television Centre for everyone to see.

He drew plans and made scale models and sketches of his design. The head would be just fractionally larger than life and mounted on a solid concrete plinth – a design not unlike that of his magnificent bronze lion's head made for the new Lions' House at the London Zoo.

We liked the idea of a canine "blue plaque." After all, if the houses of famous figures could be officially identified, it was equally fitting that a famous television star should be honoured in the same way.

Petra had undoubtedly made history, and as she had come and gone through the Main Gates of the BBC's Television Centre every week for almost the whole of her life, what better place for Tim's bronze than just inside those gates – next to the Blue Peter Tree and the box we buried for the millennium – which includes her photograph as well as those of Patch and Jason.

Petra was loved not only by us, but by millions of others. In terms of the sheer pleasure she gave to children and adults in a turbulent and often frightening world – she truly *was* "a dog for everyone".

First published in Great Britain by
Pelham Books Ltd
52 Bedford Square
London WC1B 3EF
1978

ISBN 0 7207 1059 6

Printed in Great Britain by
Ebenezer Baylis & Son Ltd.